Wealth T

From The Wicked To The Righteous

Dr. Daniel Daves

Mighty Eagle Publishing
www.mightyeagle.com
P.O. Box 179
Mansfield, TX 76063
682-651-5501

MIGHTY EAGLE PUBLISHING

ISBN: **0989591913**
ISBN-13: **978-0989591911**

A GOOD MAN LEAVETH . . .

Prov 13:22 A good man leaveth an inheritance to his children's children: and the wealth of the sinner is laid up for the just.

God has made it plainly clear through the bible that the house of the wicked will fall *(Ps. 37:28, 91:8, 129:4, Prov. 3:33, 10:27, 14:11, 21:12, Is. 14:5)* and the wealth of the sinner is laid up for the just.

As we learn more about the Kingdom of God, His dominion over the heavens and the earth, and His sovereignty over mankind, we will see that God is directing the affairs of men – even making way for the wealth of the fallen system of man (Babylon) to be brought into the hands of those who serve Him and love Him. He has a purpose in bringing this wealth to His beloved, an eternal purpose of provision and supply for His saints.

God desires to meet the needs of mankind, and for each individual to trust Him to take care of every area of life. However, many people live in direct contention with this divine order, fighting pridefully to build his/her own little kingdom through the strength and wisdom of man – leaving God completely out of their life's picture. This type of lifestyle is called wickedness in the bible. *(Wickedness is generally translated as adverse or wrong living; harmful or hurtful, displeasing decision making, or missing the mark.)*

God (our heavenly Father) wants to meet our needs as we trust in Him. But He also wants to prosper us abundantly, as we reach into a new realm of faith and willingness. Many people are called by God to the wonderful lifestyle of giving. As we accept that calling and life-style, He will begin to give abundance to us (His vessels) so that we can pour this abundance out on those who are in need. He is looking for ambassadors who will take up His purposes, and help those who are sick and need help.

Mat 9:12   But when Jesus heard that, he said

unto them, They that be whole need not a physician, but they that are sick.

Here is a little story. Two men sat and prayed, "Our Father who art in Heaven, hallowed be thy name, thy kingdom come, thy will be done on earth as it is in heaven. Give us today our daily bread…" Suddenly, two loaves of bread came out of Heaven and were given to the one man, but nothing was given to the other man. The man with two loaves went on his way and said, "You keep on praying brother, and God will somehow give you some bread too."

WRONG ANSWER!!!!

The Lord gave one man two loaves to meet both of their needs. The man with two loaves had a divine opportunity to become a broker for Heaven, and deal out the supplies to the one in need, having his own needs met as well. Unfortunately, because of greed or incorrect teaching, this man with two loaves missed his opportunity to become an ambassador from Heaven. He will be judged for his greed, and the other man will suffer because of the first man's decision. How many people are suffering needlessly today? How many times did you call out for help in your past and thought that God didn't hear your call? Most likely the answer was as close as the two men in the story above, and greed held your answer back from you, not God.

Oh, that we would hate greed with a vengeance for the pain it's brought, and tear it away from our lives!! This action alone would stop so many people from undue suffering.

God is looking for people who will help establish His covenant on this earth. He has many who are praying to Him with realistic needs, and He is sending qualified ambassadors with the goods from Heaven. Ambassadors from Heaven must be tested, tried and found faithful in the little things. After loyalty and faithfulness is found in a person, then comes the Heavenly supply for the multitudes, because –

Matt 25:23 … thou hast been faithful over a few things, I will make thee ruler over many things:…

You and I must be tested for faithfulness. God is watching to see what you do with your one or five talents. Be rest assured, if you won't give to the poor or tithe to your local church now, you will never be faithful over much if it were given you. But if you can trust God enough to stand on His word and use what you do have to help others, He will increase you as you pass the testings of faithfulness and loyalty.

Prov 11:24 One man gives freely, yet gains even more; another withholds unduly, but comes to poverty.

and…

Prov. 11:25 A generous man will prosper; he who refreshes others will himself be refreshed.

When you pass tests of faithfulness, you will be given more talents and widespread ability to become a bigger blessing. As you increase and grow, God reminds you:

Deut. 8:18 But thou shalt remember the LORD thy God: for it is he that giveth thee power to get wealth, that he may establish his covenant which he swore unto thy fathers, as it is this day.

We must understand and believe that God wants to bless you, but not so that we can hide our prosperity away in barns for ourselves only. God's prosperity will allow you to take care of your needs, and even better your lifestyle. But our lifestyle must not be in high priority. His purpose must always remain first, and then He will give you the desires of your heart. Many people fail the test after they are given limited supply of supernatural funding from God. They forsake the original agreement and resort back to greed – holding on to the new found wealth and storing it up in newly dug cisterns (personal agendas).

Jer 2:13 "My people have committed two sins:

They have forsaken me, the spring of living water, and have dug their own cisterns, broken cisterns that cannot hold water.

A certain man began to prosper in his business. But instead of acknowledging God and helping others in his new found prosperity, he built bigger barns to store his blessings. This man's actions revealed him to be a fool and a wicked man.

Luke 12:16 - 21 And he told them this parable: "The ground of a certain rich man produced a good crop. He thought to himself, 'What shall I do? I have no place to store my crops.' "Then he said, 'This is what I'll do. I will tear down my barns and build bigger ones, and there I will store all my grain and my goods. And I'll say to myself, "You have plenty of good things laid up for many years. Take life easy; eat, drink and be merry." "But God said to him, 'You fool! This very night your life will be demanded from you. Then who will get what you have prepared for yourself?' "This is how it will be with anyone who stores up things for himself but is not rich toward God." (NIV)

If our hearts are true to Him, and we are a true covenant people who are resolved to helping establish His covenant on the earth as yielded vessels of mercy and blessing, then we are sure candidates to receive the wealth of the sinner for the building and increase of God's kingdom!

Isa 9:7   Of the increase of his government and peace there will be no end.

Mat 11:12   And from the days of John the Baptist until now the kingdom of heaven suffereth violence, and the violent take it by force.

HOW DO I RECEIVE THIS WEALTH?

Many Christians believe that the wealth of the sinner is laid up for the just, but seem to have a stubborn, incorrect theory that they'll get it at the end of time. Beloved, you won't need the wealth of the sinner at the end! This world's wealth has no comparison to heavenly treasure, and the scripture clearly states that earthly treasures won't be found in Heaven! *Mat 6:19-20 Lay not up for yourselves treasures upon earth, where moth and rust doth corrupt, and where thieves break through and steal: But lay up for yourselves treasures in heaven, where neither moth nor rust doth corrupt, and where thieves do not break through nor steal:*

Mat 6:21 For where your treasure is, there will your heart be also.

POSITION YOURSELF

If you are going to experience the wealth of the sinner, you must position yourself to receive it. A person can quote the scriptures all day long, and go to his grave never having received the promise of God. This person never positioned himself to receive the blessing. Positioning yourself takes faith in action. Faith without works is dead, and likewise belief in God's promise must bring about an action (response) to the believer, or the scripture/promise will never have life in it.

We bring the promises of God to life in us when we mix the promise with our life and action.

First, you must take an inventory of yourself. You must see clearly that you may be out of position at this time to receive a greater measure of the wealth of the sinner from God. You are limited right now to receiving wealth from God in only a few areas, some being:

Your job or occupation, a personal business, your church and spiritual family, your natural family, neighbors, email or your mail box "miracle" events that may come your way.

As an alcoholic must come out of denial before help is possible, so must a person come out of financial and impoverished denial before he/she can receive help from God.

Many people are patiently waiting for God to drop a miraculous one hundred pound block of gold out of the sky into their back yard…

… and prove me now herewith, saith the LORD of hosts, if I will not open you the windows of heaven, an pour you out a blessing, that there shall not be room enough to receive it…

The good news is that this will never happen! God is not a heavenly Santa Claus who throws gifts down the spiritual chimney because we quote a scripture and yank His chain. He's not a "Bless me" machine that operates on two AA scriptures and a voice command. He's making it all together clear that He doesn't give pearls to swine *(Matt. 7:6)*. God does however; open the windows of opportunity to His servants! He opens the floodgates of supply through heavenly vision and inspiration. He does show his children the river of supply and how to tap in to it. He wants you to position yourself for the blessing.

The life-style that you now live is the same

life-style that you will be living 20 years from now, unless you position yourself. Your checking account figures will never dramatically change, your savings account will grow at the same rate, and your giving abilities will not drastically change – so get used to it! It would be foolish to try to change your financial condition without being willing to make any changes in your lifestyle or daily habits. It would also be foolish to try to lose weight without changing your exercise or daily food intake. Coming to these conclusions in your life will cause you to be prepared to Position Yourself to receive the wealth of the sinner. Remember, if you make no changes to your current position; expect no changes from God in the future.

Note: Some people who are hard headed and who dislike change will end up moving forward to some degree anyway through hard times and a lot of needless suffering. God sometimes must dry up a persons' brook and cut off their supply of meat (Elijah) in order to get a person to move forward into His will.

Don't be one of these that has to 'move or die'.

THERE IS A RIVER!

There is a river of finance, supply and blessing that is flowing past you every day. This river of supply is the wealth of the sinner. It's close enough to you that you can touch it if you reach out to it. This river is supplying nations, culture groups, people in your city and even your neighborhood. The supply is virtually unlimited, only to your understanding, your faith and the perspective of the person who is willing to tap into the river. This river is flowing into the pocket book, bank account and hands of the sinner today, this very moment as you read this booklet.

WHERE IS THIS RIVER? I CAN'T SEE IT?

As you step into your car to go to work today, you will notice a little subdivision of houses being build. That builder is a hard working man who loves to build homes. He makes around 30% profit while building these. It's great for him. In about ten - fourteen weeks, he can build a turn-key home and bring in anywhere from $40,000 - $100,000 profit. What a life!! As you continue on, you'll notice a road crew building a new bridge on the highway *(Ever wonder how much a bridge costs?)*. These companies make a good profit. *(Have you ever price a crane or bulldozer?)* By the way, the owners seldom come out to the construction site.

A little further down the road, you stop at your favorite convenience store for a donut and a tank of gas. While you're there, you get a ticket for the car wash and a daily newspaper *(along with 600 other people that day)*.

You notice a pink Cadillac in the parking lot, and smile as you think of the nice lady who must sell Mary Kay cosmetics to her friends and clients. *(Man, she must sell a lot of eyeliner to afford that car!)*

Then you arrive at work in your car *(ever wonder how much the car dealer really made on that sale to you?)* and sit down at your desk. Everything around you is associated with the river of supply – from the chair you're sitting on, to the desk, the computer, the phone, the mail, pencils, paper, the building you're in, the floor that your feet are resting on, the coffee the you're drinking, etc… Each product or service used and/or consumed was manufactured, distributed, shipped and paid for – completing the cycle of wealth transferal from one hand to the other. This was accomplished by the divine enterprise of exchange.

Question: What do you currently exchange for your wealth?

You ask yourself, "Why am I working at this job?" To pay your bills and supply your family, of course. You are trading your life's time for an hourly wage that you have settled and agreed on. *(By the way, how much money does the bank make on that home mortgage and your new car loan?)*

Lunch time brings you to the little restaurant down the street, or to the vending machine in the break room. After work, you stop by the grocery store and hand them hundreds of dollars every month to supply your family with an ongoing supply of food and beverage. And the list goes on and on...

Get the picture? Even while you and I are driving to church on Sunday morning, your home town McDonalds is netting $10,000+ today selling breakfast muffins, burgers and greasy fries. The grocery store will net thousands, and that Wal-Mart store will make $40,000 - $70,000 profit today because of a great sale and good weather!

Beloved, we are OUT OF POSITION!

Lu. 16:8 ..for the children of this world are in their generation wiser than the children of light.

These   business   owners,   bankers,

manufacturers, builders, distributors and sales people have positioned themselves for the river of wealth to flow in to them. This ought not be! Why does the river not flow to you and I? Because we are not in position to receive it.

FAITH NEEDED SOME ASSEMBLY REQUIRED

Repositioning yourself will take hard work, blood, sweat and tears, some education and a radical change in life style and belief. Your faith in action will take time to build and perfect as God leads you on a new road.

Prov. 3:5   Trust in the LORD with all thine heart; and lean not unto thine own understanding. Prov 3:6   In all thy ways acknowledge him, and he shall direct thy paths.

The Lord is a dominion oriented God, with plans to bring all kingdoms under His dominion.

...The kingdoms of this world are become the kingdoms of our Lord, and of his Christ; and he shall reign for ever and ever.

If this is the mind of Christ, then we are commanded to take up this same mind. No longer can we wait for Him to come pull us out of this world's mess and give the planet over to the devil, but we must occupy until He comes, and violently take the kingdom of Heaven by force!

Phil 2:5 Let this mind be in you, which was also in Christ Jesus:

Your renewed self is going to become a giver, a mercy oriented blessing to those in need, to your community and to the local church. God will help you to position yourself, and you will help God establish His kingdom on this earth.

Prov 11:24 One man gives freely; yet gains even more; another withholds unduly, but comes to poverty.

Prov 11:25 A generous man will prosper; he who refreshes others will himself be refreshed.

You will be making some radical changes in your lifestyle in order to position yourself. You will be:

Buying and managing businesses, reaching out to people with your product/service, purchasing real estate, working from sun up till sun down and then eight more hours. You will be stepping into areas that you've never dreamed of, trying new ideas, investing your money, time and talent, sacrificing your times of relaxation, learning to invest in the stock market and taking up a new position of promise

You may ask, "Is this biblical?" The Word of God is full of principled examples. When the Israelites entered the promised land, the manna *(supernatural daily supply)* ceased. The priests had to take a step of faith into the flooded banks of the Jordan before God stepped in and parted the waters. They had to march around Jericho for seven days, then they blew the trumpets and shouted before God brought down the walls. After that, they had to go in and finish the job, killing the enemy in Jericho after the walls had fallen. The Israelites obeyed and worked and God brought the necessary reinforcement. It was a joint venture, a co-mission, a COMMISSION IN THE LAND OF PROMISE.

Today, you and I are called to the great commission of Jesus Christ. We have a world to reach with the gospel so that God's covenant will be increased on this earth to mankind. This co-mission will take a budget of trillions of dollars, finances that the church does not have control of today. How will we get control of it? We won't, unless we position ourselves to get it.

The promise is ours, given by God. He has promised the benefits of a co-mission to us. In other words,

Deu 31:6 ...for the LORD your God goes with

you; he will never leave you nor forsake you."

Heb. 13:5 ...for he hath said, I will never leave thee, nor forsake thee.

God will help you! He will open doors for you and part rivers for you when you step out in faith into this river of supply. Who should receive the profit from the sales of fuel, clothing, automobiles, cosmetics, houses and lands, food and consumables? The righteous or the sinner? Of course, God wants to bless the righteous!

YOU CAN LEAD A HORSE TO WATER, BUT YOU CAN'T MAKE HIM DRINK

Many horses aren't really thirsty enough for water to take it in when the opportunity comes their way. However, there are a few thirsty horses out there that are being called to the river of blessing!

MANY CHRISTIANS ARE AFRIAD

OF THE RIVER BECAUSE THEY DON'T BELIEVE THEY CAN SWIM

Many have never been taught to swim in deep water such as this. God is calling you to deep waters, where your feet don't touch. You may be fearful of even the thought of jumping into this fast moving stream, knowing that the commitment of a jump will carry you down stream to a place beyond your control. (*Read Ezek. 47:3-5*) Some people are afraid of the thought of actually controlling large sums of wealth, and would rather be controlled by wicked men who will write a weekly paycheck in return for precious hours of their life given in labor.

Please understand that I'm not against a person working for a company and receiving a paycheck for time worked. But I do believe that there are great treasures in you that will allow you to rise from secretary to office manager, then further – from mailroom worker to executive vice president, then further. Don't settle for you current position

– shoot for the top! God will help you and will train you.

1 John 2:27 But the anointing which ye have received of him abideth in you, and ye need not that any man teach you; but as the same anointing teacheth you of all things, and is truth, and is no lie, and even as it hath taught you, ye shall abide in him.

IS MONEY WICKED?

Some people feel deep down inside that large sums of money will send a person to hell, and that money is the root of all evil. Don't buy the big lie!

1 Tim 6:10 For the love of money is the root of all evil:

If your purpose for inheriting wealth is to establish the kingdom of God among men and to be a faithful ambassador of His supply, then it's clear that you are in love with God – not money. Remember –

Mat 6:24   No man can serve two masters: for either he will hate the one, and love the other; or else he will hold to the one, and despise the other. Ye cannot serve God and mammon.

Things are not always as they seem on the surface. There will be many people in Heaven who have had great wealth, and there will be many people in hell who never had an extra dime to their name! If you love God first and serve Him, He wants to bring you into wealth to establish His kingdom, because –

Mat. 7:11 …how much more shall your Father which is in heaven give good things to them that ask him?

The love of money will bring poverty to an individual. Many rich and poor people in this world are full of poverty solely because of their love of money. This however, is not our motive for prosperity and wealth!

THE RIVER FLOWS BY US TODAY!

Will you position yourself? Are you ready for change? Will you open yourself to the opportunities that God has made available to you? Will you say, "I just can't do it", or will you say –

Phil 4:13 I can do all things through Christ which strengthens me.

Decide with me today that you will not be willing to go to your grave broke and impoverished, never having seen the promise of God as a reality in your life. Make immediate plans to position yourself for increase!

CHANGES ARE COMING!

You will be making many life changes soon. Your occupation may change, your work hours may change, your living quarters, home address, city and state may change. Your dress code and your schooling may change. You will begin to make actual progressive steps of change towards positioning yourself by faith in Him who's called you into this river. Eventually you will begin to see your finances change. That's right! The finances will be one of the last things to change after you've successfully positioned yourself to receive them.

YOU GET WHAT YOU SETTLE FOR

What you currently have is what you've currently settled for. Don't settle for where you're at any longer! Get up, decree a change, and go to work positioning yourself accordingly!

Job 22:27-28 Thou shalt make thy prayer unto him, and he shall hear thee, and thou shalt pay they vows. Thou shalt also decree a thing, and it shall be established unto thee: and the light shall shine upon thy ways.

What do you need? What does the kingdom of God need? What does your church need? What does your neighbor or family need? Set some goals, and covenant with God to build His kingdom and to become a vessel of heavenly supply. Position yourself, work hard in your co-mission, and experience the new river of blessing as it begins to flow to you for dispersion in the areas of God's destiny in your life.

BE A BROKER FOR GOD

I know of a missionary in Mexico who gives over a million dollars per year to other missionaries. He says, "I'm just God's broker. He gives it to me and I give it away – and I live somewhere in between." Once you've begun to position yourself, finances will come! Now comes the thrill of working with God, establishing His work in the earth through the local church and your destined mission. Where do I sow it? That's another book.

Remember –

Prov 13:22 A good man leaveth an inheritance to his children's children: and the wealth of the sinner id laid up for the just.

Dr. Daniel Daves
www.doctordanieldaves.com

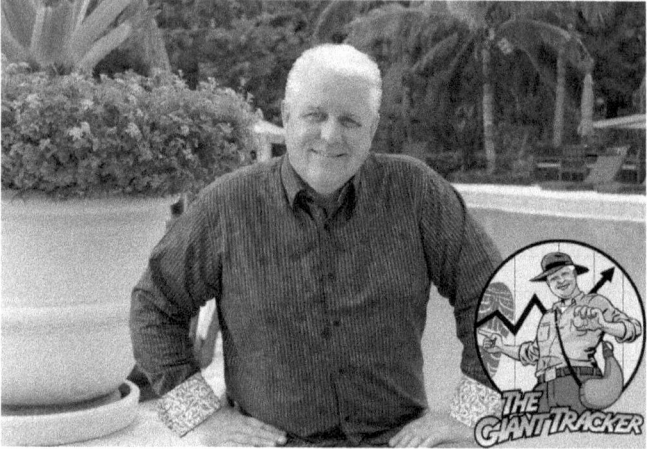

ABOUT THE AUTHOR

Dr. Daniel Daves is an author, conference speaker, innovator, mentor, and business advisor. His focus is building successful systems of multiplication and training faithful men to follow their dream while pursuing Christ in every area of life. He is particularly versed in non profit programs, business acquisition & expansion, creative design, advertising and media development. Dr. Daniel has written various books and training materials including a stock market trading system that utilizes the rhythm and cycles of God. His most important work to date, the "COMPASS GUIDE" one year core life training system for success which helps a person to find God's direct purpose for their life.

Dr. Daniel holds degrees as follows: Masters of Missiology, a Doctorate in Ministry (D-Min) and a PhD in Christian Business Administration from Logos Christian College & Graduate School, Jacksonville, FL. He is a certified open water diver and private pilot. He enjoys playing keyboard and guitar and has recorded five music albums and multiple music videos in his younger days.

Dr. Daniel's passion is the third world and being a voice to little ones who have no voice while helping to caring for their nutritional, medical, and educational needs. He is currently involved in commercial greenhouse growing technologies and multiplying food growing in hardest hit areas of the third world. He currently lives with his wife Tracy in Panama where he oversees Central American children's programs in Costa Rica, Panama, Honduras, Mexico & Guatemala. He also helps investors to integrate their international investments into credible and growing industries.

We recommend that you subscribe To Dr. Daniel's free newsletter from his web site at www.doctordanieldaves.com . Join a live "COMPASS GUIDE" seminar at a city near you and meet Dr. Daniel personally as he pulls God's designed destiny out of you in a single one day session. If you want professional mentoring in trading all markets, Dr. Daves will teach you how to trade technically using five of his "close to chest" power trades which names he has trade marked because of their high percentage of success! He teaches everything in his six month bi-weekly online training classes.

Global Food Providers

The clarion call to produce food for those hungry and in desperate need. "Food is power. Whoever has the food has the power!"

Contact us to help support a rural community leader or church planter who needs to start a farm to feed the hungry and "at risk" orphans and widows. Our online agricultural college will help train leaders around the world for total community transformation!

www.globalfoodproviders.com

Children's Feeding Network

A USA 501(c)3 non profit organization reaching out to "at risk" children in Central America, Philippines & the USA.

You can donate to any of our greenhouse projects, feeding programs and agricultural college for community leaders through Children's Feeding Network and all donations are tax deductible.

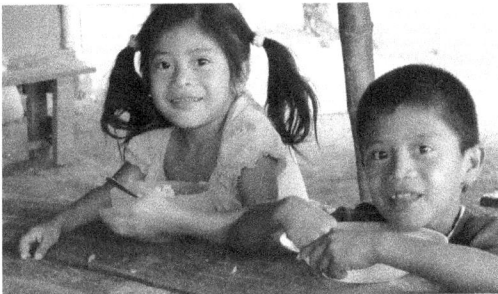

www.childrensfeedingnetwork.org

AIDS Research & Assistance Institute

A non profit 501(c)3 organization reaching out to African children with AIDS/HIV and those with immune system challenges. You can ship a 5 gallon bucket of life saving Flax Hull Lignans which will keep 15 orphans healthy for one year, for $1,040 shipped.

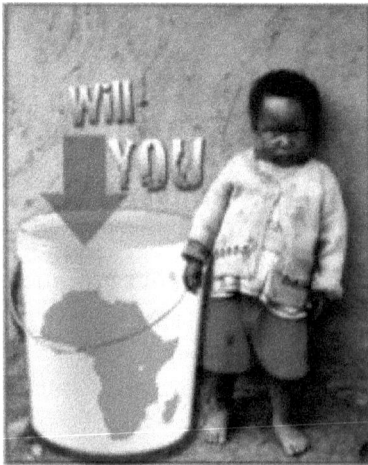

Nutritional Bucket Donation
$1,040.00 Per Bucket Shipped
(Feeds 15 Orphans For One Year)
Donate Below - Thank You

www.aidshivawareness.org

Books available through Mighty Eagle Publishing at www.doctordanieldaves.com .

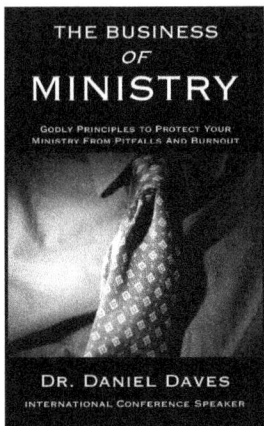

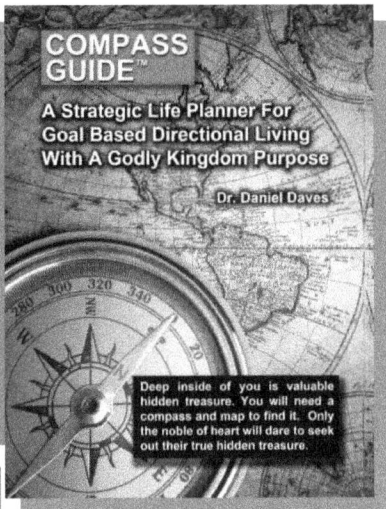

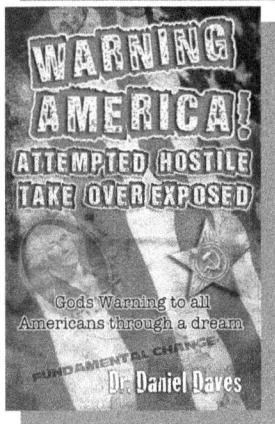

Compass Guide: Eng./Esp. Learn 13 ancient secrets of goal setting intermingled with prayer to find your true purpose in life.

The Business Of Ministry: Eng./Esp. Learn critical ministry keys to keep yourself from burnout when pastoring a church or leading people in general.

Warning America!: Eng. America has experienced a hostile take over from within as she shudders in her faith. Learn how to identify the enemies of your freedom and your children's future, and position yourself accordingly. Protect you faith, family, finances and future. This book tells it all from the perspective of two godly dreams that Dr. Daves had in 2008.

www.ingramcontent.com/pod-product-compliance
Lightning Source LLC
Chambersburg PA
CBHW070722210326
41520CB00016B/4428